Acknowledgments

No book comes to fruition without help. My thanks to Jennifer Froelich for her expertise and very helpful suggestions; Susan Leach and David Carrozza for their time and perspective in reading early drafts; my good friend Brent Phillips for his thoughtful analysis and review; and to my traveling companion and brother in spirit Tack Chumbley for his professional help and advice.

But more than these, I am inspired and indebted to those people I have known through the years who have handled overwhelming grief and devastating loss with a grace and faith that is uncommon to many today. The example these special people have left for me, and others, has enriched my life and reaffirmed the anticipation for our magnificent tomorrow.

Dedication

A year or so ago, several of our family and friends were hit with a series of tragic losses. It seemed that everywhere we turned there was unexpected death and terminal disease.

Earlier, some very dear college friends shared a wonderful and similar experience with my wife and me - we each had new grandsons named "Henry." One night their little Henry had a fever and stopped responding. Henry was buried a few days later.

Our Henry is still with us. The pain and guilt I felt for this family prompted me to do something more than just say, "I'm sorry."

Steve and Marilyn…this is for you.

Additional copies can be purchased at Amazon.com

CONTENTS

PREFACE

You're living life as best you can, making decisions you believe will ensure happiness for a long time. Life is moving along as expected when all of a sudden you are blindsided by some catastrophic news. You knew that disease or death was always a possibility – but not a probability. Now it's a fact. This tragedy is life changing.

What went wrong? Well, life went wrong. Please understand, not just your life, but *all* of life has gone wrong. The world we want doesn't exist. There is no perfect life. There is no perfect marriage. There is no perfect family, because there are no perfect people. Yes, there are many good people in this world, but sin has afflicted it in a devastating way and it will never be what we would like it to be.

A world of justice, where evil is always defeated, a world of safety where evil is always kept away, and a world of joy where evil never interferes, doesn't exist…and it never will in this life. People in this world can be violent, unfair, and evil. Evil can assault the innocent and the guilty go unpunished everyday. This is the cold hard reality of life.

It may be of little comfort to some to learn that this kind of world is not what God wants either. It may be harder still to accept that this world is not even what God originally created, but this is the fact of the matter.

Differences of theology aside, go to the Petrified Forest in Northern Arizona and see the miles of evidence of the previous world left behind. Once great rain forests and life-teeming swamps are now as barren as some fossilized, cosmic parking lot. Look in either direction for a hundred miles or more and see canyons and mesas with the unmistakable marks of stone-crushing water flows, large water flows that mark mountains all the way to the top. Fly over the Southwestern United States and see from above the massive watermarks from an ocean now long gone; they're everywhere.

Something big happened. Bigger than any world war. Bigger than any revolution. Bigger than anything modern man has experienced. The original world of Genesis 1:1 is gone.

Sin has disastrously trumped everything. Man's sins have set a fatal course for this world, and we're all caught in it. No one will escape death.

A Brief Word to the Doubter

I will not argue for the existence of God in this book; the fact is, either you believe or you don't. I will observe a few things from the Bible about the nature of God, but I am not obligating you to accept my conclusions. If you reject the idea of an omnipotent God ruling in heaven, that is your decision and there is little I can say to comfort you.

Not that I don't want to, I am truly sorry for your heartbreak and loss, but you will see in this book that no earthly power can undo the reason for our grief. I'm not being fatalistic in saying this. A powerful consequence is at work.

You may dismiss my position as simplistic or the expected belief of a "Christian" but I ask you to hear me out. Neither of us (you nor I) can fully understand, much less control the world. If you doubt this, consider the following examples:

- Unprincipled, unethical, and immoral law-breakers (sinners) are in every walk of life. When these people achieve powerful positions in government, injustices happen that most are powerless to control. Innocent people get hurt and killed, even slaughtered. Unholy wars devastate whole generations, yet these wars continue.

- It is no different in organized religions. All manner of evil was perpetrated in the crusades. There was nothing "holy" about them. The innocent have always been vulnerable to the wicked, and organized religion has done more than its share of evil.

Whatever you may believe or reject about God and Christianity, I want you to see that sin, human sin, is the provoking factor in all the evil around us. This world has been hijacked by sin, and everyman has a part in it because every man has sinned. Even the best among us have violated some moral law at one time or another. It has been said that the definition of death is to suddenly stop sinning. Like it or not, we live in a world that is suffering from sin's accumulative effect.

But is this is the reason my little child died? Somebody else sins, so my child must die? What about children in war-torn primitive countries? They didn't sin. They didn't do anything to deserve their suffering. How do believers in God reconcile such evil with their faith in a good God?

I am writing this to both believers and nonbelievers because tragedy and death show favor to no one. All men share in this universal experience and every one of us cry. Every one of us wants an explanation and needs some reassurance about this life.

Empty words never heal. Words need truth behind them to have any power to effect change. The words of this book have a reason behind them.

Hear me out. We are going to find some hope.

INTRODUCTION

Life can be brutally violent in a split second.

Your only child, the child you have been so careful to monitor what he ate, where he went to school, whom he was with, and what he was learning, is now in high school. He rides with his friends to the football game on a Friday night. He and his friends are sitting at a red light when a drunk driver rear-ends their car. Everyone is seriously injured, but everyone will survive...except your child.

Your spouse has to run an errand across town. She stops at a convenience store and walks in on a robbery. She is shot and killed as the nervous thief runs out of the store.

News like this comes and we're stunned! What? What just happened? What did they just say? No, this must be a mistake; but we're told there is no mistake.

Immediately we go on some kind of autopilot. We are going through the motions of living but have no idea how we are doing it. Momentarily, it seems we may even have to remind ourselves to breathe. Everything seems to shut down and stop.

These are scenes from a kind of hell that no one wants any part of, yet these things happen every day. When these unexpected horrors invade our life, we often look up and indict God with the charge of fraud. *"If you were truly a God of love, you wouldn't have let this happen. You can't be a loving or just God if you allow such evil to assault and destroy innocence."*

While we may not be ready to abandon our belief in God, right now our faith is staggered and we just can't see any hope in front of us. How do we reconcile our horrific loss with this merciful God we have always heard about and may have believed in, but now have serious doubts about? How could this indescribable nightmare be a part of any good or righteous plan of God?

What could God be thinking?

Why would God permit this?

God, do you know what this has done to me?

This book is not an attempt to defend God. He doesn't need my measly defense. In approaching this subject we are all treading on holy and dangerous ground. We will need humility and patience as we try to navigate our hearts through such sadness. To believers, we will listen to His Word, but it will not be like before. Now we're hurt, confused, and a little angry – maybe very angry - at this sudden soul-shaking change in our lives. Pain has a way of fogging the mind and skewing our judgment. We'll need time to stop, think, and absorb God's reassurance when we find it.

To the unbeliever I offer a few thoughts and a personal observation, which I hope will help you. I'm not trying to force any religious faith upon you. You have reasons for your convictions, and I will leave you to decide what helps you the best. I will simply look back at a few things written long ago that speak to the pain that all men have shared at times like these.

> *For the thing I greatly feared has come upon me, and what I dreaded has happened to me. I am not at ease, nor am I quiet; I have no rest, for trouble comes.*
>
> Job 3:25,26

It is my hope this little book can be of some solace to everyone whose wounds are still torn open and bleeding.

Kenny Marrs
January, 2014

CONFLICT

WITH

LIFE

And in the wreck of noble lives,
   something immortal still survives.
                              Henry W. Longfellow

Chapter 1

Oh The Humanity

*Man is born of woman and is of few days
and full of trouble. He comes forth as a
flower and fades away.*

Job 14:1, 2

I often find myself in an airport waiting for flights, and I sit watching hundreds, then thousands of people walking by. I wonder: Who are all these people? Where are they coming from and where are they going? What kind of lives do they have? What kind of problems are they facing? Some look worried, some annoyed, some anxious, and some look carefree. From all over the world, they come and go, carrying with them their story.

A famous movie from 1948 begins with the words: "There are eight million stories in the naked city, and this is one of them."

Every person is a story. Not all are as exciting as some, and not all are as tragic as some; but every person has a story that is so…human.

Do you think there is any human experience that is genuinely unique? I think not. From the most wonderful to the most horrendous, it has all happened to man…repeatedly. Not to diminish your joy or demean your sorrow, but the fact is that we can feel nothing that hasn't been felt before, and likely not nearly to the extent of some.

Everyone Celebrates, Everyone Cries

Everyone can handle good news; it's when we suddenly encounter a tragedy that we're momentarily paralyzed and don't know what to do. The amazing thing about mankind is its resiliency. In spite of the horror or injury or injustice, most people find a way to recover and go on. Mercifully, life is fluid.

When playing with other children, a crippled child does not think of himself as afflicted. The pursuit for him is pure joy, and for just a moment…he achieves it. He may not be able to run, but he can laugh. He may not be able to jump, but he can shout for joy. He may not be able to ride a bicycle, but he can enjoy life as full and as exciting as that of any other child.

There is an important lesson here: joy will be found in our minds, not in our bodies. True happiness will largely come from within us…not necessarily from around us.

We tend to become more cynical and pessimistic with age. We never hear of a "cranky young man." The troubling thing is that with time and circumstance, some personalities can wither and sour. What a sad sight. We become what we choose.

We may be mourning a great loss now, but in time we choose whether or not to *continue* grieving. If we're not careful, we can let this sorrow poison every tomorrow.

The Bible says there's a time to weep, a time to laugh, a time to mourn and a time to dance (Ecclesiastes 3:4). We've heard this before in a song, but just what does it mean?

It means there's a time for everything in this life, and we need to recognize and accept it.

Life is not one channel. Life is like cable TV - the plan with every imaginable channel under the sun. The variety is great, but the problem is we don't have full control of the programming. The channel can suddenly switch without any warning and we find ourselves watching something in our lives we don't want to see. Worse, we can't change the channel until this show is completely over. We are forced to witness things in life that we didn't choose and are powerless to stop.

When a tragedy assaults your senses and you can't (or don't want) to shake it from your mind, remember, your story has been told before. You are not the first to feel this kind of hurt. Your story isn't unique, your story is human.

In a world measured in millennia,
we control about two weeks.

Chapter 2

Why?

*How long? Will you not look away from me,
and let me alone in my saliva? Have I sinned?
What have I done to You?*
Job 7:19,20

One of the most powerful cinematic scenes in a modern movie was the graveside scene in "Steel Magnolias." A young woman dies leaving behind a husband and infant son. The mother wants to know why her "little girl" had to die. When she is told by a friend that her daughter is now safe with Jesus, the mother says yes, that should be a comfort, but it isn't. She wants her daughter back here…with her…now. Like an exploding volcano, the mother then erupts and all of her grief, anger and rage come spewing out.

This is the reality. This is exactly how we feel when someone we love has been suddenly snatched away from us. We were powerless to stop it, desperate to reverse it and now as the reality sinks in, we're filled with a type of righteous rage that screams: *Why?*

"I don't understand. Why did this horrible thing happen? I know things like this happen to others. I see and

hear of them everyday, but here? In my family? To us? To me? Now? Why?

"Surely this isn't right. My loved one was not a threat to anyone, they were good and loving, the kind of person this terrible world needs more of. There are plenty of lawless people alive right now that should have died in their place. If there was any real justice in this world, this wouldn't have happened."

"God, if You…"

Wait a minute. Did we just say "God?" What's going on? What are we doing?

Here is where we almost instinctively start reaching out; reaching out for someone we hope can *do* something about our loss.

We have heard all our lives about a benevolent God who watches over the innocent. Well, where is He? We need someone who can do something about this right now. We want to go back and somehow correct this crisis. We need someone who can push a giant reset button.

God, can't you do that?

The doctors and medical staff have shown their limitations; after all, they're just human. They mean well and would restore my child or my spouse if they could. But now I need their supervisor, someone who is over them, someone who is over…everything.

We pray. We may privately plead; we may beg and promise, but after a while it sinks in: our loved one is gone and nothing will change that.

Slowly, painfully, we come to the realization that God is not going to answer our prayers…at least not the way *we* want Him to.

We may discover biological reasons for a specific disease, human error for an accident, or an evil source for an assault, but nothing in this earth can explain why our loss is so, random, and irreversible. We feel as if we just lost in a giant lottery of death. There were so many other people to pick, but death chose us, and there was nothing we could do about it.

We're empty. We need something to fill us. We look around but can't find anything that satisfies us.

We need something to carry us through this day, something to quiet our spirit at night, and to prop us up again the next morning. Doctors may prescribe a sleeping pill or antidepressant, but these won't take away the staggering fact of our loss. We eventually have to wake up and then relive the pain all over again. We're in a dark place.

We need something else. We need peace of mind. We need a kind of peace that can take control.[1] We need a kind of peace that is able to get inside and calm our heart, because all this world will offer us is the raw reality of our unrecoverable loss.

Yes, counselors and authors tell us to cherish the memories and fill our minds with the good things we remember. But is that it? Is just a nostalgic look *back* all that we are left with? Fond memories have their place, but we want something more. We need something to look *forward* to. Yesterday was sweet, today is painful, but what about tomorrow?

When we get past the initial trauma, we start searching for a rational, logical explanation for why this happened. Who can give us some answers and provide a plausible scenario for a meaningful future?

Someone mentions Jesus…but what has He got to do with my loss? I've seen the movies and know the story, but those things happened almost 2,000 years ago; how is this relevant to me today?

I know what some of you may be thinking: "I don't need religion right now, I've heard about Jesus all my life and I might even believe the story of Jesus, but right now His name is just a word to me. He is not doing me any good at the moment and He is certainly not bringing my loved one back."

Keep reading. We're going to find some answers for today *and* tomorrow.

Footnotes

1. Philippians 4:6,7 - *Be anxious for nothing, but in everything by prayer and supplication, with thanksgiving, let your requests be made known to God; and the peace of God, which surpasses all understanding, will guard your hearts and minds through Christ Jesus.*

As a child we looked to a parent or other adult who demonstrated a benevolent authority over us. These people made us feel safe. We trusted them to take care and protect us from whatever threat may be looming just outside our world. That is why we obeyed them.

I know that for most of us, not being anxious is easier said than done, but there is a "truth" to our "trust" in God. In a highly vulnerable moment, we can lose our direction in life. God can guard us against this kind of unraveling when we put our trust in the words of Christ.

Those who are familiar with the Bible may recall one of the descriptive titles of Jesus as:
"The Prince of Peace" in Isaiah 9:6

Suffering can only be noble
when its purpose is true.

Chapter 3

Does Suffering Have a Purpose?

In the day of prosperity be joyful, but in the
day of adversity consider: Surely God
has appointed the one as well as the other,
so that man can find nothing after him.

Ecclesiastes 7:14

No. Suffering has no purpose. Suffering is senseless. Suffering is pointless. Suffering assaults and drains a living being of every drop of energy, happiness, and life. Suffering is the most cruel joke life will ever play on us. And once we begin to suffer, it never stops. Life becomes burdensome and we doubt the worth of any further living. It's over.

Suffering is so unfair we want to scream it to the world:

I don't deserve this. I want everybody to know
the pain I am going through - but don't think
you can understand it, nobody knows how I feel.
Just stand back and feel sorry for me.

There...feel better?

Now that we've got that out in the open and off our chest, we've lowered the pressure. We can exhale the immediate pain and anger. We now have some room for thought.

Let's look at this question again. Can there be a purpose in suffering? Can my suffering result in something good? I can't see it now, but does that mean I won't see it later? I don't believe it now, but does that mean it doesn't exist?

Some Christian authors have tried to tell us that suffering is our "friend." This seems a little too cute. I know that suffering has tempered some men and women to hold a greater faith, but suffering still takes its toll. Burdens can strengthen, but if we're not careful, chronic burdens can tear down.

We've been taught to look for the silver lining in the dark clouds of life, but sometimes its just not there. Losing your husband or wife to cancer does not make you a better person. How on earth could losing your child or grandchild to leukemia be good for you? These ideas seem absurd.

Understanding that mortal life on this planet is flawed with sin and as a result is sentenced to disease and death, may help us with a greater perspective, but that doesn't give us any comfort. We need to look closer if we're to find any meaning.

We are all struggling with the sentence of death, but what is the point of suffering? Someone mentions that even Jesus had to suffer before He was crucified. But wait, didn't Jesus suffer for a *purpose*?[1] Yes, Jesus died to save men from their sins; and the lawless cruelty of His beatings and execution exposed the sheer evil of sin that continues to assault good men today.

However, today when we suffer disease and death, we do so as sinful men who are subject to a sinful world. That's a *reason* not a purpose.

To discover reasons we have to look back. To discover a purpose, we often have to look forward.

I recently heard of a Christian woman, who had been diagnosed with terminal cancer, tell her believing friends not to ask God for her to be cured. Instead she asked that her friends pray to God that He would show her a way she could use her illness to help others. This took an extraordinary foresight and faith that no doubt opened a door to discovering her purpose.

When faced with our own mortality, it begins to make great sense to seek a purpose, rather than writhe in self-pity. This may be one of the closest things men can do in their lives to emulate Christ.

The fact is, the terminally ill can have a sharper focus and perspective of man's mortality.

The death of an evil man usually brings relief to people; but the death of a good man is different. People will remember, appreciate, and learn from the truth and beauty this good man brought to their world...especially while he lives and speaks with this sense of purpose. Who wouldn't be blessed from personally knowing a life (and death) like that?

Suffering, Patience and Peace of Mind

Even if we can't see it yet, there is a biblical principle found in the New Testament that speaks of patience being the result of enduring troubles and trials.[2] A unique patience that will bring a calming peace to those who have survived repeated burdens, trials and afflictions. In time we discover that the longer the affliction, the greater our endurance; the harder the trial, the deeper our spirit will grow. Our troubled spirit can walk through a door into a genuine peace.

Amazingly, we can look and see people all around us who are hurting, yet they continue to smile. Even more, recall the stories we've heard about families with an afflicted child. The testimony of parents and siblings talking about the love and strength they received from the afflicted child will often surprise the average person. Now yes, some marriages and families can crumble under the pressure of special needs children, but others seem to adjust and thrive. How does this happen? What alters these hearts to become so patient with tragedy and feel such gratitude for their burdens?

There is something remarkable about our nature that can take the tragic in stride and move on to future days. Like a flowing river, our family and friends have a way of picking us up and floating us down stream at the speed of life once again.

Please understand, I am not saying there is *necessarily* some good or profit in your suffering; but you may discover a new purpose or, a new opportunity in this struggle. Don't give up on life - doors can open.

Your suffering may seem pointless and cruel right now, but as long as flowers bloom and babies are born, there are more days ahead that have a promise of future joy for both you and your family

Footnotes
> 1. 1 Peter 2:21: "Christ also suffered for us, leaving an example that we should follow in His steps."
>
> Today, we may rarely be physically persecuted for our faith, but we do suffer in the body and inevitably die. In death we fall victim to this flesh, reminding us all that we are following in the way of Christ. Jesus had to die, but He also had to be raised from His grave to accomplish His mission of deliverance. Jesus did not intend to *stay* on this earth, He planned to go home and take us with Him. Our resurrection from this life, like His, is our way home. Read Romans 6:1-14 for a more complete explanation of this crucial principle.
>
> 2. James 1:2,3

A strict belief in fate is the worst kind of slavery; on the other hand there is comfort in the thought that God will be moved by our prayers.

Epicurus

Chapter 4

No Rhyme or Reason

But if not, then we shall know that it is not
His hand that struck us; it was by chance
that it happened to us.

1 Samuel 6:9

One of the most difficult truths of life is that sometimes, accidents just happen. It is no one's fault. Life is such that we can indeed be "at the wrong place at the wrong time."

In our lawyer driven world today, every loss is somebody's fault. Someone's neglect, incompetence or greed allowed a condition to exist, which caused our friend or family member to be injured or killed. Someone is responsible for my loss and someone must pay.

There are some Christian writers who espouse the belief that *every* accident and catastrophe comes from the immediate hand of God and is a direct judgment upon the victims for their past sins. This, however, is just not the case.[1]

Almost 3,000 years ago King Solomon grappled with this question and stated:

I saw that the race is not to the swift, nor the battle to the strong, nor bread to the wise, nor riches to men of understanding, nor favor to men of skill; *but time and chance happen to them all.* (Ecclesiastes 9:11)

Sometimes in life, there is no specific reason for what happens; but time and chance just happen. Good fortune can happen to the undeserving and calamity can come crashing down upon the innocent. This does not mean that all of life is mere chance. Clearly there are events we witness that have a definite cause and effect, yet at other times it is sheer coincidence that something did or did not happen to us.

On September 11, 2001 this nation was assaulted. Almost 3,000 people died as a result of a political and religious fanaticism that every sane-thinking person would identify as evil. These evil men did not know who their victims were and did not care. They were simply intent on killing as many Americans as they could. This is an extreme example of how organized religion will morph to follow a human agenda.

There are thousands of stories here. No doubt many family members of those who were lost, and many who were spared have asked why this happened to them. Why did they happen to be in that building on that morning? Why did they happen to take that flight and not another? Others would ask: Why didn't I go to work in that building that morning? There are thousands of scenarios but they all come down to Solomon's recognition that time and chance happen to them all.

Divine Control?

Nowhere in the Bible do we read where God the creator, micro-manages all of His creation. Natural and spiritual laws have been established and the whole of the universe functions within those laws.

However, tragedies don't mean that God is unaware or unconcerned. Jesus tells us that not a sparrow falls to the ground apart from the Father's knowledge. God is aware of every detail of our life, even to the number of hairs on our head.[2] Peter tells Christians to cast every care upon God, because He cares for them.[3] Consider this carefully: God knows *and* He cares, but He will not suspend natural law to prevent earthly tragedies; His focus is on eternity.

Your loss may be accidental. If so, remember: Ecclesiastes **9:11** -time and chance…

Footnotes

1. This is nothing new. Many of the Jews of the New Testament believed this. Jesus, however, refuted this belief in Luke 13:1-5.

2. Matthew 10:29-31

3. 1 Peter 5:7

*If I thought I was going to die tomorrow,
I should nevertheless plant a tree today.*
                                    Stephen Girard

Chapter 5

The Sobering
Facts of Death

*It is better to go to the house of mourning
than to go to the house of feasting, for that is
the end of all men; and the living will take it
to heart.*

Ecclesiastes 7:2

The problem we have with death is that it is so final. No amount of grief counseling or prayer will bring back our loved ones. Nothing. There were still lots of things we needed to do with them and say to them, things to discuss and plan and enjoy together. But now they're gone and we'll never see them in this life again...ever. We will never again hear them laugh or feel their embrace. Their life is gone and the world doesn't even seem to notice.

Other people die in wars. Other people die in accidents. Other people are murdered, but not us, not our child, not our husband or wife. We are good people. We help others. We comfort others. We're not supposed to be the ones who need comforting. We don't want to be pitied by others, yet the fact is that death has come to us and we're not prepared. We knew it *could* happen but didn't believe it *would*. Now that it has, we struggle with the finality of it all.

Today, the immediacy of life has imposed its own importance upon us in a way that makes the fact of death intolerable. Not to ignore the trauma of death, but we need to see the bigger picture here.

Vanity of Vanities

King Solomon had wealth and wisdom beyond any man. He was troubled by the inequities[1] and seeming emptiness of a short life and set out to find what profit, if any, man could gain from living "under the sun." His findings are recorded in the Old Testament book of Ecclesiastes.

After indulging in all manner of pleasure, then considering wisdom and justice, seven times in this book, Solomon will conclude that there is nothing better for a man "under the sun" than to eat, drink, and enjoy the fruit of one's own labor.[2]

Consider his seventh statement concerning life "under the sun:"

> Live joyfully with the wife whom you love all the days of your vain life which He has given you under the sun, all your days of vanity; for that is your portion in life, and in the labor which you perform under the sun. Whatever your hand finds to do, do it with your might; for there is no work or device or knowledge or wisdom in the grave where you are going.
> Ecclesiastes 9:9,10

A closer look at the message of the book will tell us that Solomon is going to view life in two different ways. The first part of the book (1:1–12:12) deals with the physical part of man's life, thus the phrase: "under the sun." The second part of the book will have Solomon stepping back and viewing life with a much broader, more inclusive lens. Solomon's conclusion to the whole matter in 12:13 reads: "Fear God and keep His commandments, for this is the whole of man."

There is a joy to be had on this earth, but this joy is temporary; death will come. The blessings of family, work, and a satisfaction of enjoying the "fruit of our labor," will not last forever. This is why Solomon uses the phrase: "vanity of vanities, all is vanity." It is not that life isn't worth living, but rather a recognition that whatever we may be able to accomplish and enjoy in this life (under the sun), will eventually pass; we cannot hold onto these things.

I understand the message of this book to say: Enjoy life. Drink long and deep of the blessings you receive in this life. Live with love in your heart. Be grateful and faithful to family and others. Remember where these things come from, and humble your mind and life to the power Who rules over all of it.

Footnotes
1. Ecclesiastes 7:15.

2. Ecclesiastes 2:10,24; 3:12,13,22; 5:18; 8:15; 9:7-10.

Tell me whom you love,
and I will tell you what you are.

Arsene Houssaye

Chapter 6

Consequence of Love

We love Him because He first loved us.

1 John 4:19

No feature of our humanity is more powerful and evident than love. We see demonstrations of this all around us. From wedding proposals at the ballpark, to an airport or hospital maternity ward where families anxiously wait with signs and balloons, to a park bench where an elderly couple are holding hands, Expressions of love are all around us.

Where do you suppose this comes from? There is nothing random about the fact that we love; we are following our created nature. This is an indelible part of being created in the image of God. We are the only creatures in the universe who love.

It is important to note that whenever a local or national tragedy happens that destroys property or takes lives, something often happens that is praised but never fully explained. I'm talking of people who open their homes, feed strangers, and offer anything needed by the afflicted. Why do people behave this way? Where do these acts of love and charity come from? They are not random.

Whether people realize it or not, they are acting upon their nature…their godly nature.

God's Dilemma

Even if you're not sure there is a God, take a minute to "think outside the box" and put yourself in the position of the Creator. We may think an omnipotent God would have no problems, but let's think again. If this God is a God of love, this will present some problems for Him. Let me explain.

Have you ever been rejected by someone you loved, a breakup, a separation, or worse - a divorce? Have you ever witnessed a loved one self-destruct? How did you feel? Helpless? Heart-broke? Unloved?

These emotions, and others, are a part of our being creatures who love. Now think, if God is a God of love, could not His heart be broken too?[1]

The dilemma God has faced is that His most beloved creation (mankind) has been sentenced to die because of their sin. Just like a concerned father, God wants to help His children, but He cannot ignore or dismiss the penalty for sin.[2] Law cannot be broken.

What can God do to rescue His children from the consequence they have brought upon themselves? Theologically, Jesus Christ answers this dilemma,[3] but we need something more than theology right now. We need assurance. We need peace. We need some genuine expression of love.

Love isn't easy for the lover. Parents caring for their small children, mates caring for their health-stricken spouse, grown children caring for their aging parents - we give a large part of ourselves to the one(s) we love.

Such is the case for our God in heaven. Why else would He go to all of the trouble, pain and cost of this crucifixion?

The most famous Bible passage in all of the world is John 3:16: "For God so loved the world that He gave His only begotten Son." Consider for a moment just exactly what this says about the power and price of God's love for us.

The magnificence of this love and its unequaled expression to the world cannot be overstated. If nothing else, the fact of God's supreme and voluntary sacrifice for us should prove He is not indifferent to our broken heart.

Divine Grace

There is an oft-told story concerning a group of scholars who were trying to define the singular distinctive characteristic of Christianity. When asked, C. S. Lewis answered: "I can answer that in one word: Grace."

The Christian story is unlike any other. What other religious faith is founded upon a God who is serving, sacrificing, and dying for His own creation?

In speaking of the crucifixion moment, the Swiss writer and composer, Jean Jacques Rousseau wrote: "If Socrates died like a philosopher, Jesus Christ died like a God."

Look around and marvel at what the power of love will move men (and God) to do.

Footnotes

1. The people of Israel repeatedly broke God's heart when they would leave Him and turn to idols. It reached the point where God would direct a prophet (Hosea) to take a prostitute for a wife. Her unfaithfulness and Hosea's sadness would illustrate the shame of Israel's sin and the depth of God's grief. Read the book of Hosea to learn more.

2. Romans 6:23.

3. A closer look at Romans 3:26 tells us how Jesus Christ is the comprehensive answer to this dilemma: *To demonstrate at the present time His righteousness, that He might be just and the justifier of the one who has faith in Jesus."*

Through the sacrifice of Christ, Law would be satisfied (God remains "just"), and man is acquitted (God becomes the "justifier"). The law is satisfied, God remains righteous, and man is rescued from his fate. This is the basis for the gospel.

Chapter 7

The Perfect Illusion

…not that I am perfect, but I press on.
Philippians 3:12

In the preface of this book I mentioned that there is no perfect life; there is no perfect marriage; there is no perfect family. Now, for those of you who may have been a little annoyed or even unsettled at that remark, let me take the time here to explain a little further.

Yes, there are many very good people in this world and there are many very good marriages. There are many who have genuinely committed themselves to their mate and their children. Their mates have in turn also committed themselves to the marriage, and the two of them have worked together to raise a wonderful family. These people have truly enjoyed life as the Creator intended.

However…

People are human; and being human we have our moments where the weakness of our flesh and/or the blindness of our ego interferes with our marriage, sometimes even foolishly pushing the marriage and family to a frightening uncertainty.

Marriage is a journey and the children that often follow are a challenge that bursts on the scene with immediate demands. These demands will ebb and flow, then will slowly fade away as the children marry and start their own family, but along the way, everyone messes up at one time or another.

Now, how do you define "perfect?" If you envision perfection as having no problems, you know this is not right. We need to think again.

Problems are inescapable, and to think we are to somehow never have a problem is unrealistic. Consider the fact that children test *every* marriage …without exception. Now when we disagree with our spouse about our children, does that mean we don't have a good marriage? - of course not.

The real issue in every marriage is not if we will have disagreements or problems in our family, but rather when these differences appear – what will we do about it? How will we handle it? More directly to our subject - what happens to the marriage and family when we suffer a sudden, unexpected, and catastrophic loss?

Times of catastrophic loss are a very precarious and dangerous time in our marriage and family; and if we have believed our marriage and family "perfect," we might crumble under the reality of our human condition. Unrealistic expectations can set the stage for a disastrous chapter in our life.

Good people will have differences of opinion with those they love - sometimes a very sharp difference of opinion. Problems can arrive from work, or between family and friends, or legal and financial matters can present a particularly poignant challenge to the very best of marriages. A variety of difficulties will come, but that doesn't mean we have a bad marriage or family. "Goodness" stands apart from being "problem-free."

The "American Dream"

We Americans have had such an extraordinary period of prosperity this past century; and that, coupled with a media-fueled ideal of the perfect life, has contributed to a unique problem. We have subtly formulated an ideal of perfection that will not tolerate any personal disaster. The "perfect life" must go as planned, with only *minor* changes.

The "American dream" may mean different things to different people, but by whatever standard we use to define it, we need to remember that an ideal is just that…an ideal. Ideals may be worthy to aspire to, and a blessing to achieve, however, life does not end if the ideal momentarily slips away from us.

When we set such unrealistic standards and extreme definitions for our lives, then, when a problem does come, or worse, a tragedy takes something/someone away from us, we feel as if we are failures; we must be bad people. Understand that prosperity simply means good fortune - *not* personal virtue. Likewise, tragic loss reminds us that we're not exempt from life - *not* that we are bad people.

Greener Grass Syndrome

Don't make the mistake of looking to your neighbor's marriage and family and thinking they have a "perfect" family because they always seem to be happy and prosperous and never seem to have any real problems.

Experience and common sense tells us that what we see is not always the whole picture. Yes, there are people who truly are happy and prosperous, but ask them how they got where they are and they will tell you of the difficulties they endured and the committed devotion to their vows. They will tell you these things, not to boast, but to help others attain the same. Prosperity may be random, but happiness is not an accident. Nothing precious comes easily.

By now I trust you have picked up on what I am saying here: Perfection is not found in the absence of problems or tragedies, but the dedication and commitment of all concerned to treat each other with the respect, dignity, and love (real love) that nurtures the spirit. THIS is what will prepare you and your loved ones to weather the storms of life. "Perfect" families will understand this.

CONFLICT

WITH

GOD

It were better to have no opinion of God at all than such an one as is unworthy of Him;
For the one is only unbelief — the other is contempt.

Plutarch

Chapter 8

"Where is God?"

Oh that I knew where I might find Him,
that I might come to His seat.

Job 23:3

Whenever we find ourselves openly questioning life's injustices, or inexplicable tragedies, or some unimaginable evil, we inevitably ask: *"Where is God?"* This question has at its root at least three components:

An admission
An assumption
An assertion

I. An Admission: There Is a God

Whether a person will recognize it or not, every idle mention of heaven is an admission that someone or something is able to hear them. People do it all the time.

No one should ever have to go to the funeral of a four year old…but it happens. When we find ourselves in this particular kind of sorrow, do you ever hear anyone say something like: "Well, that was unfortunate but that's life." Of course not. To say such a thing would be so insensitive and offensive to the family that many would lash back in anger. Why? Because no parent would ever think that his or her child didn't matter in this world. To assign the death of a child to simply being a matter of fate is unacceptable to our way of thinking. There has to be a reason and a purpose for our child's existence, doesn't there? Surely, a child's life means something; and not just a child's life, but every life. Right?

Where do we find the reason? Who can give us a definitive answer? In times like these, almost all men have looked to heaven. Why?

Nature itself declares an authority that is beyond this world.[1] This kind of power cannot come from any person or place on this earth; such power must transcend the world. Let me put it another way: Name one government that can control the weather.

From ancient times until now, man has battled disease, famine, flood, and each other. In times past, when a crop was withering or a village was endangered or a loved one stricken or any other manner of impending jeopardy, men would offer a sacrifice.

To whom? Other men? Of course not. They needed a greater power than men. And while we're on the subject, where did ancient man get the idea of an animal sacrifice in the first place?

Men today may ignore, even forget God for long periods of time, but the irony of mankind looking to heaven in times of personal tragedy is so universal, it's stunning.

Instinctively, we *know* there is something greater than this planet.

II. An Assumption:
God is either impotent or indifferent

When a believer is faced with a moment of loss that cannot be logically processed, they wonder how a God of love can be a part of this. Ancient philosophers have argued the problem of evil and God for centuries. From the highly suspect *Epicurean Paradox* to modern day best-sellers, these have all proposed that we have only two options: either God wants to help us but can't (He is impotent), or He could help us but won't (He is indifferent). Unable to accept the latter, many have concluded that God is a good God who sympathizes with man in times of evil but is powerless to prevent it.

With all due respect to those who have devoted much of their life to this question, neither of these are a solution nor a consolation. This is reminiscent of a nation's leader saying, "I feel your pain." What good does that do? How would an impotent deity give me any hope? This is like a pat on the back from my losing attorney as the police lead me off to prison after I have been convicted of a crime I didn't commit. This is not the answer.

If the idea of God being helpless to help were true, how could we possibly reconcile this with the belief that God created and controls the heavens? In other words, are we to believe that the author and director of a precise solar system and the most complex forms of all life is unable to control disease or disasters? This makes no sense.

To conclude that God is willing but powerless to help man is an assumption that maligns the *nature* of God. To conclude that God is able but unwilling to help man is an assumption that maligns the *character* of God. Both of these ignore a truth that is in fact the real answer to these dilemmas. We will study this answer later in chapter 14.

III. An Assertion: God is not worthy

Here is where Satan does his most effective damage to mankind. From Genesis to the Revelation, from Eve to Job's wife, the devil from the beginning has used every circumstance he can to indict and defame God. When Satan told Eve that she would not die (Genesis 3:4), he was putting in her mind that God could not be trusted because He was lying.

You will never find in scripture, tradition, myths or legends, Satan trying to convince the world that God does not exist.[2] The devil is evil, but he is not stupid. He knows who God is. He has walked in the presence of God. He has argued and fought with God. God cast him out of heaven. He knows God's power and rule, yet he ceaselessly rebels against God. His jealousy of God is so consuming, he will destroy anyone or anything (including himself) to satisfy it.

This is the setting for the temptation of Christ in the fourth chapter of Matthew. The devil is desperate to manipulate heaven and earth into his favor. Men have been easy foils (they will worship anything) but the Son of God was different, He resisted the devil's bribe and Satan was forced to leave defeated.

Yet, the devil continues to deceive the world, and his lies can be powerfully effective.[3]

Job's wife ultimately accepted the devil's premise that God was not worthy of her praise, but deserved only her cursing.[4] The devil has always tried to misdirect man away from Jehovah's goodness. Men need to understand that this is the ultimate objective of Satan and evil. *Any* spiritual alternative is fine with the devil as long as it is not centered on the true God in heaven.[5]

Today is no different than in ancient times. The lie of Satan continues with every tragedy.

Today we worship life. When mankind suffers, people are all too quick to charge God with every evil motive. Many survivors of horrendous wars and unspeakable inhumanities have struggled with this; some are so scarred and angry that they cannot forgive God for allowing such tragedy to happen to them.

Interestingly, as angry and bitter as some men may become, almost all will not deny the existence of God...they still need someone to blame. If there were no God, who would these people be angry with? Evil needs a face for angry people to attack.

Tragically, here is where we can become unwitting emissaries for the devil.

Hurting and angry hearts are a ripe field for the devil to sow his seeds of contempt and bitterness toward heaven. At a time of catastrophic loss, we need to understand that if we allow ourselves to simmer in our anger, we can drift over to a very dangerous precipice.

Rationalization leads to justification. The reason so many are quick to indict God is that somehow, in people's thinking, this gives them a logical or valid reason to withhold any submission to God's will. It's the perfect excuse. The thinking goes like this: because God would allow such a tragedy, I am not morally obligated to regard or obey Him.

How convenient. Things are *God's* fault, not mine. God was in control, not me. I wanted nothing but peace for all men; but war and pestilence and death have happened all over this world and I had nothing to do with it. Since God would allow this to happen, He really doesn't deserve my consideration.

Now where do you think this kind of thinking comes from?

Notice that even today, angry critics don't deny the existence of God, just His goodness. Religion is a favorite target of critics, and organized religion is a favorite tool of the devil.[6]

But wait a minute, just because an evil man uses the name of God as his justification, does that make God culpable? Let's be honest about this.

The sad irony is that no one has been slandered more throughout history than the God who made us and loves us.

Still, some may angrily ask: "Where was God during my tragedy?"

The answer to this is that God was in the same place during your tragedy as He was during *His* tragedy…when His Son was murdered.

Footnotes

1. Romans 1:20 tells us that the evidence for God's existence and His manifest wisdom in the created nature is so compelling that man has no excuse to deny his Creator.

2. James 2:19: "even the demons believe and tremble."

3. 2 Thessalonians 2:9-12 - The context is the explanation of a future apostasy that will affect the entire church. Within this warning is a description of how great and far reaching is the influence Satan can have upon man. While the power and wonder of his lies will be unprecedented and unequaled on the earth, the key to his defeat is the love of truth. Some how the devil will wrap his lies with an element of pleasure (pride?) that will blind those who do not truly seek the truth.

4. Job 2:9.

5. It is interesting that some theologians have noted that the philosophy behind polytheism was that it was a way for some cultures to accept the calamities that came to them. Each god was limited to their own specific realm, which excused the other gods.

6. Organized religion can very subtly lead people away from the Lord. The focus of faith becomes the *denomination*, not Christ. A person will believe and behave at the dictate of the "church" and not the word of God. It is a very old but little told story.

Chapter 9

Did God Do This?

*Does it seem good to You that You should
oppress, that You should despise the work
of Your hands?*

Job 10:3

Our child is born with Down syndrome, or some
other crippling disease. Did God do this?

Here is where we need to be careful. Life gets
complicated with tragedies, and we feel compelled to
find definitive answers to every crisis. Sometimes we
will decide it's our fault when family afflictions are
severe. God is punishing us for some past sin.

Am I being punished for something I did? Is
God testing me? Is God arbitrarily picking on me?
Has someone in my family sinned, and now I am
paying for it? I'm a good person and not mean or
disrespectful of others (as far as I know), so why has
God done this to me, to us?

Can this somehow be my fault?

Medically, we may track the DNA of people
and determine the probable cause of certain
abnormalities. Sometimes couples are tested and

doctors advise them to not have children because the combination of their specific DNA has a high probability for some type of defect that could be passed on to their offspring.

But wait a minute - haven't we already seen that this whole world and everything in it is defective? We're all defective in some way or another; some defects are just more visible than others. People are born everyday with bad eyes, bad teeth, bad bones, bad skin, bad brains, bad hearts, bad livers, and bad lungs. Defects are everywhere. It is amazing that life continues as it does.

Why would we only question God about the major defects but not the minor ones?

I know this may be of little comfort to some, but we shouldn't be surprised when defects (of any degree) come to a sin-cursed world. The consequences of our sins are all around us. They will never go away. This is why the message of the New Testament is deliverance *from* this world rather than deliverance *for* this world.

We are utterly foolish to declare to the world that God can't or won't do something. We don't know. God is not a man whom we can scrutinize and define. God is in the unique position to be able to do anything He wants anytime He wants. We can't control God.

Because the Lord will not cure my cancer doesn't mean that He is indifferent or impotent. God did not cause cancer. God may not *need* to cure cancer for His eternal plan.

Diseases and maladies are just a part of the reality of a sin-cursed world. Again, this is not the world God originally created. God does not want His creation to suffer the traumatic episodes that injure and destroy that which He loves. *We* are the culprits. *We* are the sinners. *We* are the ones who chose to throw away His original world of peace and life. If there is one thing we all are forced to agree upon, it is that this world is fatal. No one will survive this world. That is why the God of heaven and earth has prepared another world that evil can't touch

Critics will call it fantasy, skeptics will call it wishful, atheists will call it foolish; but who among the unbelievers has an alternative? Am I to believe that I should live a moral life that in the end will have no more meaning than a cockroach? Why all the effort from famous unbelievers to convince us there is nothing beyond the grave? If they're right, they're wasting our time *and* theirs. Nothing matters.

I readily admit that I do not know why our Creator does what He does, but I believe I will see Him face to face when I leave this world. He doesn't need to answer to me, I will answer to Him.[1] Furthermore, as strange as it may sound to some, this is what gives me hope. The fact that I will face my Creator might give me pause, but it also encourages me that one day I will see and hear what this life was all about. I will see Him in all of His majesty, and will then understand the mysteries of His triune glory.

And wait a minute, while we're talking about this, did God promise us a pain-free life? Did He promise that we would never grieve or suffer affliction? Did He promise that life would always be comfortable for us, and our families?

Now God *did* promise to save us, but did He ever tell us that we would never be touched by evil or misfortune? No. Then why do we act as if God has broken a sacred promise to mankind? When tragedy comes to our house, we are being wounded by a horrible consequence that long ago came to a sin-infested world. We shouldn't be surprised.

If you look closer at many of the passages that modern day "feel-good" evangelists quote for a prosperous life here and now, you will find the context of a spiritual deliverance for a spiritual nation of God's people.

The promise of restoration and the picture God gives to the Old Testament prophets is of a *spiritual* kingdom that would never be destroyed.[2] The citizens of this kingdom would never suffer (spiritually), never starve (spiritually), never mourn (spiritually) and never die (spiritually).

Where in the New Testament do we read of the disciples of Christ living lives of physical peace and prosperity? To the contrary, disciples in the first century were driven from their homes, imprisoned, beaten, tortured, and even executed.[3] Why then do we think that everything will automatically become peaceful and wonderful for the person who trusts and follows God?

I fear that some may become so angry toward God when they suffer a loss, that they may never be able to objectively see this sinful world for what it is doing to all of us.

God has not ignored or betrayed us with the physical traumas that come to us, He is preparing a life away from this pain, sorrow, and death. He is preparing a life for us *away* from this world. This world is not our home.[4]

Real peace will be found elsewhere.

Footnotes
1. 2 Corinthians 5:10.

2. Daniel 2:44.

3. Hebrews 11:35-40.

4. 1 John 2:15-17.

*Our sense of sin is in proportion
to our nearness to God.*

Thomas D. Bernard

Chapter 10

The Consequence of Sin

For in the day that you eat of it,
you shall surely die.

Genesis 2:17

The Bible is the only reference source that tells us definitively where death came from and what it is. Death came to man because he violated law (sinned) and was separated from the presence of God.[1] Death is the separation of the body and spirit.[2] Spiritual death will be separation from God.

We understand that each man is responsible for his own actions. However, God also tells us that while the son will not inherit the *guilt* of the father's sin, the *consequence* of a man's sin can be felt for generations.[3]

Let's clear this up right now, we don't want anyone to misunderstand. We don't have to be guilty of sin to feel or even pay the consequence for another's sin. The consequence(s) are not evil...the sin is.

For example: a young father robs a convenience store and is sent to jail. The young mother and child will have to deal with the consequences (emotional, financial, social, etc.) of his sin. This young mother must now work two jobs to survive, and her life will never be as it was before. The grandparents must take care of their new grandson, and their health is failing. Everyone in this scenario suffers consequences, but there is only one sinner in this story: the young father.

Taking up this story a few years farther - the little boy grows up without having a father in the home and has no real discipline. He is in and out of trouble, and at age eighteen he rapes an underage girl. He goes to jail, the girl goes to a social worker and the new baby goes to a foster home. Now *more* people suffer consequences. A single sin can grow in its scope to affect so many and even set the stage for further sin.[4]

We may argue about specific shortcomings or breakdowns in this family, but that is another subject for another time. What we want to see here is how so much tragedy can come from just one sin. Before we assign blame to God, we need to take a longer look in the mirror. Often, prolonged family turmoil can be traced back to some ungodly source.

In a similar fashion, the world today is writhing in the distress of the sin that afflicts it. Earthquakes, floods, famines, and hurricanes were not a part of man's first home in Eden. There was no cancer, leukemia or Alzheimer's in the Garden of Eden. Further, there is no indication that these maladies would have eventually shown themselves in the garden, if man would have stayed there and lived long enough. Sin closed the door on an earthly paradise.

When Adam and Eve sinned, things changed. Things changed in this world for everyone and everything in it. Later, worldwide sin ultimately reached the point where the Lord destroyed the earth with a flood that literally changed the face of the earth. Man would no longer live for hundreds of years, and the animal kingdom would now fear man.[5]

Front and center for every man is his sin. God could no longer see past man's sin, and had to do something about it. The solution for God was the sacrifice of His Son. Notice that the solution was not *from* this world but would have to come *to* this world. The solution would be to call men away from this world, away from the sin that stands between God and every man who rejects Him.

Yet to this day we are all still living with the consequences of sins past and present. Cancer can come to anyone. Diseases affect every family, and we will all succumb to the inevitable weakness of this body. Tornadoes rip through communities leaving a path of carnage. Earthquakes rumble through crowded cities, collapsing buildings and roads, destroying life and property without distinction. The earth is convulsing with the consequence of its sinful inhabitants.[6]

We are all citizens of a world that has run off the rails and is heading for a fatal crash. No one is able to jump off; we'll all ride it to the end.

This is why *real* hope must come from beyond this world.

Footnote

1. Genesis 3:23; Romans 6:23.

2. James 2:26.

3. Ezekiel 18:20: "The soul who sins will die. The son will not bear the guilt of the father, nor the father bear the guilt of the son."

4. The little boy that grows up without a father does not inherit the sin of his father (robbery). He will suffer the *consequence* of his father's sin, but he will not inherit the responsibility or guilt of his father's sin. He will however be responsible for his *own* sin (rape). Read Ezekiel 18 for a more complete explanation from God on this subject.

5. Genesis 9:2.

6. Romans 8:20-22: "For the creation was subjected to futility, not willingly, but because of Him who subjected it in hope; because the creation itself also will be delivered from the bondage of corruption into the glorious liberty of the children of God. For we know that the whole creation groans and labors with birth pangs together until now."

CONFLICT

FOR

GOD

It happens that evil always pursues the good; the good rarely seek the evil.

Chapter 11

Did God Create Evil?

*For You are not a God who takes pleasure
in wickedness, nor shall evil dwell with You.*
Psalm 5:4

The difficulty with this question, in part, is that we are trying to define a parameter for something that can only exist in the mind of a free-will creature. While evil is manifested in the things that people do, it develops and resides in the minds of the men who are drawn to it.[1]

Evil is neither matter nor being; rather, it is a state of rebellion against righteousness. It is thoroughly against and is without any consideration for good. Evil is the culmination of everything that is against God. Contrary to the teaching of original sin, evil is not a fact in the newborn child. A newborn child cannot decide to do evil, much less know what evil is. All he knows now is discomfort and hunger; recognition of right and wrong will come later.

The Bible says that *foolishness* is bound up in the heart of a child, not *evil* (Proverbs 22:15).

It has been argued that because every man is born with the *capacity* to commit evil, therefore, evil is inherent in each man. This does not follow. You may have the capacity to murder, but that does not mean you will murder or even have the desire to murder. Just because one man may commit an evil act, does not mean that every man has that same evil desire. Evil, like prejudice, is learned, not inherited.

Evil is a mindset that is cultured through rebellion and repeated sin. In the beginning, the God who created Adam declared him to be "good." Adam would later injure his moral condition by his own willful sin, but evil was not a part of man's original nature.[2]

The solar system can never be evil because it is under the absolute control of its creator. The animal kingdom can never be evil because it is under the absolute control of its creator. All of these have no choice, but there is one exception to the creation...man.

Man is the only creature with the power of choice. From the Garden of Eden to the present, man can choose between good and evil.

God did not create evil. God knew what evil was and warned man about it, but He did not create it. Evil would be the resulting consequence of men abandoning God and His law. God stepped back and allowed His human creatures to choose evil through their self-willed sin, but God did not afflict or force evil onto man.

Evil exists and proliferates where God is not held in esteem, that is, where men reject God's authority and willfully practice things in violation of God's law. Evil is a toxic blend of immorality and rebellion that will poison and kill the soul of man.

Though God did not create evil, He has used evil for His purpose at certain times.[3] The story of Joseph in Genesis 45 is a case in point. After Joseph was betrayed by his brothers, betrayed by his employer and then betrayed by a fellow prisoner, he was put into a position to counsel Pharaoh with God's plan and thereby save the world from famine.

Joseph was used. He did not become angry, but had extraordinary insight into the ways of God. He later proclaimed to his brothers that while they meant their act of betrayal for evil, God used it for good.[4] This certainly does not mean God approved of an evil deed, but rather, He used the evil deed to bring about good.

Evil is a problem for us today because we live in it, are affected by it and cannot escape it in this sin-soaked life; however, we must understand that evil is not a problem for God. God will use evil at certain times for His purpose and when He's done with it, He will destroy it.

Christ tells us there will be an end of evil when the devil and his angels are cast into the "everlasting fire."[5]

Evil came to this world sometime after the creation and will end with the conclusion of time.[6]

Your child was not lost or killed because they were evil. Jesus speaks of humility and innocence in Luke 18:16 when He says: "Let the little children come to Me...for of such is the kingdom of God." Your child was innocent...*and God knows that.*

The height of evil irony is the devil trying to convince people that God has killed His own children, because He (God) is evil. The fact is that God has even given of Himself on the cross, that He might remove evil from His family.

Satan is the *driver* of evil. The Lord will be the *destroyer* of evil.

Footnotes
   1. Proverbs 23:7: "For as he thinks in his heart, so is he." Proverbs 27:19: "As in water face reveals face, so a man's heart reveals the man."

   2. Consider Genesis 1:31: "*everything* that God had made was *very good.*" There is no place for evil in this passage. Evil had to come *after* the creation in Genesis chapter 1. The question of the origin of evil has at its root the fact of the devil's original nature as good, but then his later rebellion and subsequent evil. When did this happen and how did God deal with this? We don't have any definitive answer as to when, but we do have the answer as to how God dealt with it in Revelation 12:7-9.

3. James 1:13 says God cannot be tempted (tested, moved, affected) by evil, nor does He Himself tempt anyone with evil. Evil has no effect upon or power over God. However, we see God allowing certain evils to unknowingly bring about good while it (evil) self-destructs.

4. Genesis 50:20: "As for you, you meant evil against me; but God meant it for good, in order to bring it about as it is this day, to save many people."

5. Matthew 25:41: "Then He will also say to those on His left hand, Depart from Me, you cursed, into the everlasting fire prepared for the devil and his angels."

6. By "end" of evil, I am referencing the fact that Christ will separate the righteous into eternal life, while the rebellious will be cast into everlasting punishment (Matthew 25:41). Read Revelation 21:8. Evil will be cast out with the rebellious sinner; it will still exist, with the devil and his angels, in a separate and contained hell of God's choosing and control. How? We don't know, but it will not be in the realm or presence of God's family.

While evil is a problem for all who are on this earth, it is not an eternal one for God's children – they will escape evil. One of the things that will make heaven what it is, will be the total absence of evil. Let your mind settle on that thought for a few moments…it is a marvelous picture.

The devil never created a thing.

Chapter 12

Is Satan Too Much for God?

I saw Satan fall like lightning from heaven.
Luke 10:18

You may be asking yourself, how on earth does this theological discussion have any relevance to my situation, or help me cope with my loss?

Good question. Stay with me.

You're reading this because you at least consider the possibility of an intelligent superior power that is responsible for your existence. This is nothing new. The Greek poet Aratus wrote the poem *"Phaenomena"* in 276 B.C. The fifth line reads: *"For we are indeed His offspring."* The apostle Paul quoted this poem in a sermon he delivered in Athens, Greece almost 2,000 years ago. This is recorded in Acts 17:28. Paul was declaring that even from ancient times, men have instinctively known there is a heavenly power that is in control. Aratus believed it was Zeus. We understand this power to be the God of the Bible.

The problem of evil is a subject that will never be resolved in this world. To fully define and understand any complex spiritual dynamic in human terms is outside our possibilities. This is not an excuse but the reality.

Attempts to reconcile God and evil have led many to conclude that Satan is co-equal with God (Dualism). This idea is not supported in the Bible. Now granted, it is a great mystery to us on earth as to why God would allow Satan a measure of power (as illustrated in Job 1-3), but this does not mean that God was forced to *give in* to the demands of an equal entity. *Co-exist* does not mean or require *co-equal*, as we will see in a moment.

I realize that hurting people need more than theological arguments. However, if we are to find any lasting comfort in a time of spiritual crisis, we need to discover and establish some fundamental, definitive truths about good and evil, truth and lies, God and the devil. Consider the following...

We read in I John 5:19 that Satan is the "ruler" of this world. What does this mean?

In Revelation 12:9-12 the Bible states that the devil was cast out of heaven and has come to the inhabitants of the earth and sea. Satan is limited in his power, but he has filled this world with his evil and lies. His objective is our death. He cannot take us by force, but he will do everything possible to deceive and entice us to sin, causing us to destroy ourselves.

Satan cannot make the sun rise or the stars shine. This universe is still in the hands of its Creator.[1] What God has done is to allow His creatures free will, while *binding* Satan on this earth. Satan has a jurisdiction that is not so much geographical as it is mental, spiritual, and temporary. Like a mad dog chained to a tree, go inside his circle of power and he will destroy you, but stay outside and you can avoid his fatal objective. We have control over our lives by our choice between good and evil, and can avoid any real threat or jeopardy because of that; yet, we must remember that Satan is in every corner of this world wielding his malignant influence, dangling a poisonous carrot in front of anyone who would be enticed. Wise men will be vigilant.

Three Passages to Consider

I make no apologies in turning to the Bible. Where else will we find proven truths that help explain man's nature and future? The "truths" of school textbooks change with each generation. For many, truth has become relative. What we need now are time-tested truths that have supported people through the centuries. No other written work can be placed next to the Bible in terms of the scope of its being endlessly scrutinized, yet its truths are consistently proven from generation to generation.

Cutting through all the centuries of traditions and legends, the only valid and comprehensive truths we have about spiritual things have come from God's revelation. The truth is, without God's revelation we would be clueless as to what is really going on "behind the scenes" in the spiritual world.

We need to go back to a time that predates any man or philosophy of man. We need to go back to the beginning. Consider the following three passages from the Bible that discuss the beginning:

Colossians 1:16

Colossians 1:16 tells us that *all* things were created by the Son of God: things in heaven and earth, things visible and invisible. Every power, every authority, every ruler in heaven was created by God's Son. There is no exception in the language of this passage for Satan.

As an object and creature of God's creative power, Satan had no choice when he was cast out of heaven, and will have no choice when he is cast into eternal hell.[2]

John 1:1-5

Here, John writes that the "Word" (manifested in the flesh as the Son of God vs. 14) was *with* God and *was* God from the beginning. Before anything was made, the Son of God was in the beginning as God. Whatever we may need to include in the fact of darkness, we are obliged to recognize John's statement that "The light shines in darkness, and the darkness has not overcome it." Satan and his evil cannot control, much less overpower the light of God.

Further, we read in verse 3 that: "All things were made through Him, and without Him nothing was made that was made." Where would Satan fit in this equation? I know of no translation that renders this passage: "All things were made by Him *and Satan*, and without Him *and Satan* nothing was made that was made." Satan is clearly a part of that which was made. Therefore we must conclude that Satan is not any kind of creator but is a part of the created.

Genesis 1:1

Genesis 1:1 is unequivocally the most sweeping statement in the Bible. Nothing precludes it (think on that for a moment). This first statement says God created the heavens (and everything in them) as He did the earth (and everything in it). There is no place for the devil in Genesis 1:1.

Further, there was a span of time from Genesis 1:1 to Genesis 3:1. The bible doesn't tell us when, the bible doesn't tell us how or why, but it is unmistakable in its statement that *"the serpent was more cunning than any beast of the field which the Lord God had made."*

Genesis 3:1 is after the fact of Genesis 1:1. The cunning serpent did not exist with God at the beginning; therefore the devil cannot be co-equal with the God who made heaven and earth. There is no room or reason for the devil in Genesis 1:1.

Though we are not told exactly how, when, or why God created all of the spirits in heaven referred to as the heavenly hosts, the Bible does argue that Satan was one of them.

So?

Right now you may be thinking: Ok, so the devil was created…why should this matter to me?

Think carefully about the alternative.

If this were true, if Satan was eternal and equal with God, we could never escape this war. Think of it like this: through all of the wars of history, innocent people have been caught in the crossfire of violence that overwhelmed their land. The citizens of an occupied country were powerless to free themselves until a power greater than the occupying force came to liberate them. Now suppose there were no greater power(s) in the world, but all nations were equal. The victimized populace would be doomed to suffer under the despotic regime indefinitely. Other armies would appear, but the war they waged would be futile. The endless fighting would never secure a final peace.

Likewise, if heaven and hell were eternally locked into an equal tug-of-war, no one could be delivered. We would be forever caught in the cross-fire of a spiritual power struggle between good and evil. We would be doomed. Our family would be doomed. Our friends and every human we know would be doomed to an eternal war where a lasting, final peace would never be realized. There would be no hope for your loved one, because there would be no hope for any of us.

However, if we have evidence that God has not only created Satan, but conquered Satan and will forever cast him out and isolate him in a place where he can never afflict man again; then we can have peace, real peace, a peace that will never be interrupted or broken.[3] This is how our hope will be realized. And isn't this what we all want…peace?

> For I am persuaded that neither death nor life, nor angels nor principalities nor powers, nor things present nor things to come, nor height nor depth, nor any other created thing, shall be able to separate us from the love of God which is in Christ Jesus our Lord.
>
> Romans 8:38,39

Footnotes

1. Matthew 5:45 "…He makes His sun rise on the evil and on the good, and sends rain on the just and on the unjust."

2. At the judgment, Jesus will say: "Depart from Me
you cursed, into the everlasting fire prepared
for the devil and his angels." (Matthew 25:41).

3. According to the New Testament, Satan is first
defeated by Christ during the temptation in
(Matthew 4:1-11). The devil moves on. When
the seventy disciples return from their victory
over demons, Jesus says: "I saw Satan fall like
lightning from heaven." (Luke 10:17-18).
When Jesus enters Jerusalem in preparation
to be crucified He says: "Now is the
judgment of this world; now the ruler of this
world will be cast out." (John 12:31).
Hebrews 2:14 states that the Son of God took
human form (flesh and blood) in order to
destroy the devil and the power he had over
death. We read in 1 John 3:8b "For this
purpose the Son of God was   manifested that
He might destroy the works of the devil."

Notice the devil and his *works* will be
destroyed, setting the stage for eternal peace.
Note also 2 Peter 3:10 where the *works* of the
earth will be destroyed as well as the earth
itself.

Chapter 13

What God Really Wants

Jesus wept.

John 11:35

A young mother is dying of breast cancer and we are scrambling to make sense of it. Her parents are horrified to think they will bury their grown child. Her husband is numb with thoughts of what he will do. What will he tell the children? What will happen to his family?

During this ordeal some well-intentioned friend or family member says something like: "We are so sorry, but this was God's will."

What? What does that mean? Am I supposed to believe that there is some kind of mysterious *good* in the termination of this life? Are we to believe that the God who gave this young woman a wonderful life with a faithful husband and beautiful little children, now decides it is better that these young children never know their mother, and that this husband must struggle in raising this family alone?

No. To the mortal mind this makes no sense; it is absurd and infuriating to most all of us. But we need to be careful here, lest we presume to speak for God in a matter like this.

Whenever people declare a death as "God's will," it is at best a clumsy attempt to console the bereaved, but in reality, we have made a huge presumption to know the mind of God in a specific case. We simply cannot know everything our Lord has purposed in every situation. We can, however, read statements in the Bible concerning God's attitude and feelings towards death.

Yes, God directed many battles in the Old Testament to strike a rebellious people, but God also said, "As I live, I have no pleasure in the death of the wicked."[1] In the New Testament we read: "The Lord...is not willing that any should perish."[2] Physical or spiritual, God does *not* want men to die. Death is the enemy of God.[3]

When I say that God does not want you or your spouse or your children or your parents or your best friend, or *anyone* to die, this is a biblically stated fact. However, we also need to remember that this Divine Being we call "God" does not exist or function within the realm of time. God stands outside of time and directs His will for eternity. That is why we must caution ourselves before we hastily presume that God is indifferent or cruel.

God warned us that if we sinned, we would die. This was not a threat but a spiritual fact of life.

This is exactly what Paul described in Romans 5:12. Death came to this world by man's sin, and death spread to all men, because all sinned. Men are not *born* with sin - they *commit* sin. *Man* brought sin to this world, not God. As a result, man must live and die with the consequences of his sin.

God had nothing to do with our sin and subsequent death. *We* have sinned, not God.

When we look closer at the Bible we discover that while man has brought the fact of physical death upon himself, God will not interfere with this law. Physical death is the sentence of everyone who ever sinned. However, spiritual death is a far more serious matter and God has done all He can to prevent and correct this death. God gave His own Son to save the world. Jesus did not die to save our bodies from cancer; He died to save our souls from hell.

Think long on this thought: God may or may not delay the inevitable demise of our bodies, but He will not allow the demise of our spirit...if we will follow Him.

If we learn anything from reading the Bible we learn the Lord's mission is to rescue and preserve life, not take it. Listen to our Lord lament over the people of Jerusalem:

O Jerusalem, Jerusalem, the one who kills
the prophets and stones those sent to her!

How often I wanted to gather your children together as a hen gathers her chicks under her wings, but you were not willing!
Matthew 23:37

Do you see this? The Lord desperately wanted these people to listen and turn to Him. He is mourning their rebellion and inevitable destruction, but there is nothing to be done about it. This is their decision and they will have to bear the consequence of it. It is not that God can't or won't save them; they have willingly and purposefully rejected any help from God. God is not culpable - rebellious men are.

Listen carefully to God proclaim His name to Moses:

The Lord, the Lord God, merciful and gracious, longsuffering and abounding in goodness and truth, keeping mercy for thousands, forgiving iniquity and transgression and sin, but who will by no means clear the guilty, visiting the iniquity of the fathers on the children and the children's children, to the third and fourth generation.
Exodus 34:6,7

We learn a vital part of God's nature in His description of Himself. The willingness of God to extend mercy and forgiveness to all is evident, however, His mercy will not interfere with justice.

The guilty (i.e. those who refuse God's grace), will be punished. Likewise the sin of rebellion will not be dismissed after a few generations. In other words, what was sin yesterday is still sin today and will continue to be sin tomorrow. The standard of morality and righteousness doesn't change with time.

This is crucial to our understanding of God. God so hates sin that He has done everything He can to redeem man from it, and has clearly proclaimed the time will come when He will destroy it forever. Yet, as long as men live, they will commit and perpetuate sin.

When this world finally does end, man will be taken from this earth, where the earth and all the sin and death within it, will be finally and forever destroyed.[4] No longer will God grieve for man's horrible fate, death will be extinguished, and all of the people who love and trust God will be gathered safely with Him forever in the home He has prepared.[5]

We cannot know the mind of God in every circumstance, but we do know that death was not what He wanted for His children. When death did come, God removed the horror and broke the hold of death in a way that man never could have imagined or accomplished. Of this, we are certain because God has said so.

Footnotes

> 1. Ezekiel 33:11.
>
> 2. 2 Peter 3:9.
>
> 3. Read 1 Corinthians 15:23-58 for a more complete explanation on the role of death in God's future plans.
>
> 4. 2 Peter 3:10
>
> 5. John 14:1-3 While the context of this statement has Jesus speaking directly to His Apostles, the principle truth of this promise is describing a place of rest for all of His disciples.

CONFLICT

CONTROLLED

Belief in a cruel God
makes a cruel man.

Thomas Paine

Chapter 14

Trying to Make a Man Out of God

Cry aloud, for he is a god; either he is meditating,
or he is busy, or he is on a journey, or perhaps
he is sleeping and must be awakened.

1 Kings 18:27

From Greek mythology to post-modern philosophies, men have repeatedly tried to bring the God of heaven down to this earth. Endless efforts to impose human characteristics and limitations on God have had their effect upon the minds of many people today.

We expect God to think and behave as we do, but without any mistakes, you know, "perfect." Ah yes, perfect...as *we* define perfect. God must only do those things that *we* approve of, and He must not require us to believe anything too impossible.

In choosing the parts of the Bible story that appeal to them and rejecting those they cannot accept, many believers(?) have concluded that the Bible is allegorical, that is, parts of it can be dismissed as fiction.

They want to believe in the Christ who taught and fed the multitude, but recoil at the idea of a virgin birth. Some will reject the days of creation, a global flood, the parting of the Red Sea, the great fish of Jonah, the existence of the devil, miracles, etc. because it all seems too fantastic to the secular mind. It has no credibility to their way of thinking.

The problem here is that the revelation of God stands in its entirety…or it doesn't stand at all. If there is any part of the Bible that misleads or misstates a truth (which God allowed to be included) how could the Lord be trusted? The inconsistency in this premise so undermines the Christian faith that if it were true, we would be doomed. If God is no better than a man who lies, what hope do we have?

However, "God is not a man that He should lie, nor a son of man that He should repent." (Numbers 23:19).

The Sovereignty of God

Men will refuse to legitimize God when God doesn't act as men want Him to. God's decisions, or lack of them, sometimes run counter to our wisdom and that is something we just cannot tolerate. We reason that God must submit to our decision(s) if we are to have any comfort, much less understanding for our loss. God must think like us.

But it doesn't work that way. God tells us:

My thoughts are not your thoughts, My ways are not your ways. For as the heavens are higher than the earth, so are My ways higher than your ways and My thoughts higher than your thoughts."

Isaiah 55:8,9

The apostle Paul explained the sovereignty of God in Romans 9:14-21. We are not in the position to question, much less control, what the Creator will do with us. This may not be acceptable to many in this world, but the fact is that God does not answer to His creation. He is not asking for our approval...He doesn't need our approval. He is simply asking us to trust Him.

Long ago, King Nebuchadnezzar of ancient Babylon (modern day Iraq), was humbled by God for seven seasons.[1] After his encounter with God, Nebuchadnezzar proclaimed:

For His dominion is an everlasting dominion, and His kingdom endures from generation to generation; all the inhabitants of the earth are accounted as nothing, and He does according to His will among the hosts of heaven and among the inhabitants of the earth; and none can stay His hand or say to Him 'What have You done?'

Daniel 4:34,35

The sovereignty of God. <u>This is it. This is the missing ingredient in most people's analysis of God.</u>

Here is where we either "get it" or not. Our world is so completely focused on this earthly life that we can't or won't consider a solution beyond our own wisdom.[2]

You see, we are not forced to decide between an impotent God or an indifferent God (as was mentioned in Chapter 8). Neither of those options will satisfy the dilemma. *The real God is sovereign.* The real God is above and beyond our thoughts and ways. The real God is ruling all creation…absolutely.

The fact is, we are all subject to the power that put us here in the first place. If our existence is pure chance, we are wasting our time trying to find answers and solutions. A logical solution will only come if there is a logical power (intelligence) behind our existence.

The Bible states that God is the creator of every man. He created the heavens and the earth and everything in them. This is where we start in our quest to understand life and death. Any correct understanding we will ever have of this life (its course and its end) will come when we acquiesce to the source that made this life in the first place.

Without God's revelation of Himself none of us would have a clue what to think about this life; it would all just be a philosophical guess.[3]

However, if we accept the Bible to be of divine origin, in both content and collaboration, we are given a window into eternity that explains the greater struggle and the reality of a victorious, eternal peace for all who will accept it.

Here's a choice for you to consider in your grief: Are you more comfortable with man being created in the image of God...or a god that is created in the image of man?

Footnotes

    1. Daniel 4:28-33

    2. Read the discussion of the "wisdom of this world" vs. the "wisdom of God" in 1 Corinthians 1:20-25. God would expose the wisdom of this world as "foolish," while the world would see the gospel message as "foolish." Amazingly, this is exactly how God wants it. "God has chosen the foolish things of the world to put to shame the wise." (v 27).

    3. Read 1 Corinthians 2:11,12 to learn how man would know the heart of God.

The Lord is in His holy temple.
Let all the earth keep silence before Him.

Habakkuk 2:20

Chapter 15

What This Means To You and Me

God reigns over the nations;
God sits on His holy throne.

Psalm 47:8

God's sovereignty trumps all other options. Regardless of the "plausibility" of a philosophy, God's word will finally rule the day because He alone is on the throne of heaven. God does not lie. He cannot be tempted. He does not favor evil. God has none of the weaknesses common to man…because God is not a man. God is eternal.

The Bible says God was present when the earth began. God has been dealing with this physical and spiritual world since the beginning. How many opportunities do you think He has had to make a mistake? Through all the centuries and the multi-billions of people who have lived, how is it that this universe is still operating?

Critics may ask: but how do you know that God hasn't made a mistake? What about all the atrocities that have happened throughout history to men? Don't these holocausts demonstrate God's failure(s)?

Answer: we've already made the point that *man* has brought sin and its consequence of death to this world. Men continue to choose to assault and kill one another; God doesn't force man one way or the other. The present moral circumstance of this world is man's fault…not God's.

But lets go further. How is it that we continue to have sun, soil and seed to produce our food? In spite of political and societal tides, how is it that a man and woman still fall in love and start families? How is it that beautiful children keep getting born? Who thought of this? Who makes this possible? Who keeps this going?

"Mother Nature" (a pantheistic expression) may provide the fruit from this earth, but natural forces don't teach us about forgiveness and love; these things come from the mind of God.

If you've been asking yourself: "What does all this mean to me? How does this help my loss?" Here's your answer…

We Need Truth, We Need Grace

The Bible says God came to this world in the flesh through Jesus Christ and that He was full of grace and truth.[1] Jesus proclaimed the objective of His mission was to forgive our sins, and then demonstrated that power by healing a paralytic man.[2] He was both willing *and* able.

Now tell me, where are you going to find a source of forgiveness that is so gracious as God? When God sent His Son to die for all mankind, He did something that is unprecedented and unmatched. No one and nothing can come close to providing such a proven and effective resolution to our sin. And the amazing thing about it is that He died for us when man didn't ask for it, didn't think he needed it, and certainly wasn't worthy of it.[3] Nevertheless, grace and truth came to our lives – together for the first time.

Peace and Love

The public crucifixion and resurrection of Jesus brought several factors into play; and ironically one of them was peace. At one time or another men have struggled with their sinful habits, their thoughts of a demanding Creator, and the seeming doom in their future. Like a lost swimmer in the middle of an ocean, men would beat the water furiously looking for a shore of forgiveness, but were never able to find it.

However, through the sacrifice of Jesus, man could now step out of this endless ocean, and rest his spirit upon the solid ground of an assuring forgiveness. Man could now find a real peace that would satisfy his soul. No more treading the waters of hopeless despair, there was now a solid shore of peace and promise to stand on. Jesus not only taught us about peace, He became our peace.

Experts tell us that in a time of crisis, we go through certain stages and need different things at different times: compassion, support, reassurance, sympathy, candor, etc., but above everything else, we need an abiding peace of mind with an assuring sense of love - love being that unique ingredient that revives the spirit and opens the heart to better tomorrows.

Honestly, where do you think this comes from?

It has come to us from our Father in heaven through His Son. Where else could we find the type of peace that transcends our earthly lives, and a love that is so purely and completely selfless? Only the God of the Bible could be the author of this love.[4]

The reality is that, all we have ever known or will know about love has come from the mind of God...not songwriters or poets.

Known for Centuries

In early world history before the printing press, scrolls of scriptures were gathered and passed around. The stories of the Bible were spread everywhere and heard repeatedly by everyone. When Bibles were later printed, they became the primary source of educational material for much of the Western world.

The basis for most early literature was the Bible. Stories of heroism, faithfulness, honor and love were founded on the stories in the Bible. The Bible has been the benchmark of character studies to authors for centuries. This is simply historic and literary fact.

The love and hope we hold for the ones we have lost is nothing new. God's message and personal example of His love for mankind has taught and inspired countless people, just like you, through the centuries with their loss.

Nothing New to God

The Bible reveals the whole spectrum of divine emotion. From God's pleasure in the creation, to His disgust with world sin; the heartbreak from His people's betrayal, to the anguish of seeing His Son murdered by the very people He came to save.

Even more, long before any of us realized we needed forgiveness, God had already experienced the heartbreak of being rejected by His children, the disgust of their sinful behavior; and yet, resolved to pay the exorbitant fine for our sins…death.

Now, who else would do this for you? Who else *could* do this for you?

The God of heaven and earth has stepped in on our behalf and provided a means of reconciliation and restitution for every man who would receive it. This means we still have a chance.

****

At the sweetest moments, life can reach inside us and gently touch our hearts. At other times, life can brutally pull our heart out by the root. These are the realities of our world, for both heaven and earth.[5]

It's good for us to remember that God's heart was broken long before ours was. God can sympathize with your loss because He's been there...and here.

Footnotes

1. John 1:14.

2. Mark 2:9-12.

3. Romans 5:8

4. 1 John 4:7-11.

5. Consider that as flesh and blood offspring of each other, nothing will replace the natural affection we have for our family in this life. This is no accident; the blessings of a family were provided for and ordained by God from the very beginning (Genesis 2:24).

It is no wonder we are so devastated to lose a family member; our love for them is more than deep...it's divine.

Chapter 16

Guilt

Can a woman forget her nursing child?
Isaiah 49:15

A brief word is needed here. Guilt is a nasty thing. It can appear from the thinnest of reasons, and afflict a person for a lifetime, if they'll let it.

Sometimes a widow or widower remarries and begins to feel guilty when they may seem happier with their new spouse than they were with their first.

A young mother loses a child and then later has another. The busyness of life and the demands of the new child take her attention. One day she remembers her first child and then feels guilty for somehow forgetting.

Often when people are able to finally put their lives back together after a great loss, they feel guilty. Any joy that comes to them seems to say to them that their loved one was not that important. They reason: I must be a bad person if I can be happy again after they are gone.

Stop this kind of thinking. Stop this run-away train before it leaves the station. If we're not careful, unchecked guilt can quickly get out-of-control and destroy us.

There are two distinct and curious ironies of guilt:

- Those who truly are guilty but have no remorse and feel no guilt whatsoever.

- Those who are innocent of any wrong, but like a mother, who, after she has sacrificed for her children, will worry that she has not done enough and sometimes will scrutinize and doubt herself to the point of debilitating guilt.

Life has a way of forcing our minds to other matters; but that doesn't mean we have lost our love for the one who was taken from us. Don't let guilt move into your mind and poison your life. Guilt has an insidious way of robbing us of all our joy, if we'll let it.

If you find yourself feeling guilty after a devastating loss, remember that as long as you are mindful (even worried) about your love for the one you lost, this is a tender testimony of your true and abiding love. You have not forgotten them, and you are certainly not an ungrateful or bad person.

Real love is patient...and that goes both ways (your loved one would understand).

Chapter 17

The Role of Faith

*Blessed are those who have not seen
and yet have believed.*

John 20:29

I had a friend named Ron who lived in Alabama. He was a successful executive accountant. He had a wonderful wife who was a talented interior designer and Bible class teacher. They had three grown children and several beautiful grandchildren. Life was good and getting better by the day for them. Ron had been asked to consider becoming a bishop in the church where they attended. Feeling he wasn't quite ready for such an important obligation, Ron declined for the time being. He told me he wanted to study more church history before he would feel comfortable and qualified to help lead the congregation. Ron was a humble and caring man.

One day Ron was mowing his yard when he had a massive heart attack and dropped dead. Suddenly, his wife was faced with all of these decisions and responsibilities she wasn't prepared for. Friends encouraged her to go to grief counseling, but she was not ready...that is, not right then. Eventually she did attend and tells a story I need to share with you.

During their round-robin discussions, the widows were encouraged to express their feelings about their loss. After a few weeks, one of the women (who was an atheist) spoke up and said, "I envy you ladies." She explained, "I've sat here and heard you express your grief, yet all of you talk of the day when you will be reunited with your husband in heaven. I don't have that hope…I wish I did, but I don't."

The Virtue of Faith

Say what you will about faith, there has been nothing in this life as powerful as faith. Prisoners of war tell of an inner strength that drove them to survive. The faith that they would be rescued or escape, kept them going. Hope sustained them, but when all hope was gone, men would just give up and die.

Critics of religion will scold people of faith as being empty-headed dupes who deserve misfortune, but ironically these same critics will walk by faith everyday. They will eat food from a restaurant not knowing where it came from, drive on the right side of the road hoping oncoming traffic will do the same, and fly in an airplane about which they have no idea if it is mechanically sound. Faith is a part of almost every facet of daily life.

For those who put their trust in God's benevolent wisdom, this trust will gradually allow the empty hole in their heart to be filled with His promise. There will be another day. The immediate shock and numbness of our loss will slowly dissipate into a grateful memory of the blessings our loved one brought to our life, and will engender a meaningful anticipation for the day when we will be reunited in the presence of our Heavenly Father.

I know this may seem a weak substitute for actually holding our loved one again, but this is something. We're not left completely empty. Do you want the memory of your loved one to always prompt anger? We will always be sad that we lost them but is this how you want it to end? Broken hearts never heal quickly and sometimes leave a nasty scar. Do you want that pain to grow and fester and darken your life even more?

If living in this world is the sole focus of our life, we will be bitter and angry when we lose the people we love. We'll never know any real peace. The loss we've experienced will rob us of any future joy, and destroy any hope we could have had…if we can't see past this life.

I know this is easier said than done. Life has a way at times of delivering a body blow that can stop us in our tracks and convince us life is over, and we will never recover from it. However, when we read of people in the Bible, and elsewhere, who suffered great loss, yet endured through their faith; we gain a hope that we can do the same.

Faith from Favor?

There is however, something here that bothers me.

When I travel to villages in East Africa and see a type of poverty that overwhelms the senses, I am embarrassed and troubled.

I have traveled to Ethiopia each year for the past 12 years. I have travelled extensively in the central and southern parts of that country. Hunger and poverty are everywhere and the occasional famine will starve people to their deaths. A few years ago a friend and I went to a remote village in the southern highlands of Ethiopia. This was a full two-day drive from the capital city. The rough dirt road turned into a path that later just ended at this village. There we met a group of about 60 people who had walked over a mountain range to meet us.

These people had earlier suffered a famine. Six of the young women had been pregnant, but only three were strong enough to deliver healthy babies. These mothers came early and met us in a private room to proudly show us their new babies and have us pray for them. The joy of that moment was later erased when I went into the gathering and saw the young women who had lost their children. They were so extremely mal-nourished that they had an eerie resemblance to the pictures we have seen of the survivors of concentration camps. They were quiet and did not speak. Famine had killed the unborn too.

My senses were momentarily stunned. I didn't know what I could say or do to comfort these pitiful young women. All the food and clothes they could carry back to their village would not fill the enormous hole in their hearts. Imagine how they must have felt when they looked over and saw the other young women who had enough physical strength and nourishment to carry a baby full term. Yet, here they were, worshipping their God.

Later the next day when we were back on the road, I just couldn't shake this image and the terrible feeling I felt. Then I remembered a few days earlier seeing four men carrying a sick woman on a wooden board over their shoulders. They were taking her to the doctor, about 10 miles away.

How could I ever validate any of my "suffering" when I have every medical and financial advantage in the world? I travel in my air-conditioned car to a state-of-the-art hospital to confer with a team of medical specialists who offer the finest treatment known for my affliction. I can buy any medication needed and hire any surgeon I want.

I may still get a bad report from my doctor, and may still be hospitalized, and may eventually lose to cancer; but I have to wonder how much the comforts of my prosperous country have affected my faith. More precisely, what is my faith really in?

A Word to Christians

Recognizing there is a superior being with the manifest power to create and control all nature is nothing courageous or particularly virtuous. In fact, it has been often argued that it takes more faith to be an atheist than a believer. The real issue here is my commitment to that faith.

The question I have to ask myself is: am I faithful to God's commands simply because I am hoping for some kind of payoff? Have I reasoned that any sacrifice I may make in this life will be rewarded with a future tsunami of blessings?

Be honest with yourself, of course you've done this. I've done this; we've all done this. There is nothing unholy or unseemly about wanting our Heavenly Father to bless us. We all want peace, love and prosperity; it is only natural to follow the source of these. We just need to remember our Lord has promised all of these in *His* home...not this one.

A Word of Caution

We also need to be careful when we are disappointed here in this life. Like some children who are pleasant as long as they get their way, but can become unbearable when they are denied anything; we too, can become spoiled in this world if we won't accept the bad things with the good. It is not that we should be stoic in the face of misfortune, but recognizing the source, duration and chance (providence?) of our good fortune in this country; we would do well to temper our perspective of this life.

We have *so* many blessings in this country, we must ask ourselves: How will my faith react when these blessings are taken away from me?

As we have already noted, nothing of worth comes cheaply or easily. The fact here is that a strong and mature faith will be a faith that has been tested...repeatedly.

* * * * * * * * * * * * * * * * * * *

By the way, my friend Ron who died in his yard...his wife's name is Faith.

What we have done for ourselves alone, dies with us. What we have done for others and the world, is and remains immortal.

Albert Pine

Chapter 18

The One Who Suffered for Us

But now, stretch out your hand
and touch all that he has.

Job 1:11

The title of this chapter may be misleading. There were actually two men who suffered for us. The most well known is Jesus Christ, but He wasn't the first man to suffer for mankind; the first man was Job.

Job is an icon. No single case of tragic loss has been more scrutinized than Job.

The frustrating thing about this story is that we are never given a definitive answer as to why Job suffered. If *we* feel frustrated, imagine how Job must have felt. He lost all of his possessions, all of his children, and then when he lost his health, his wife scolded him for his faith. Job's friends came to comfort him but ended up indicting him for sins they believed he must have committed to deserve such suffering. No one was with Job. Job felt isolated, abandoned, and then he hit bottom in chapter 7 of the book of Job. Job lost his family, wife, friends, and then it seemed he lost his relationship with God.

We can all sympathize with the frustration, and yes, the anger that Job felt when it seemed there was no reason, no explanation, and no end to his suffering. *Why God? What have I done to deserve this?* Job feels he is being toyed with by God and complained "...in the bitterness of my soul." (Job 7:11).

Adding to his frustration were his three friends whom he called "miserable comforters" who kept insisting that he had done something wicked to deserve his suffering. Job honestly protested each accusation from his friends by saying that he would know if he had done anything wrong to deserve such suffering. Job doesn't disagree with his friends' premise, just their conclusion. Yes, he should be punished if he had committed some great sin, but he had faithfully served God and could not find anything of the sort in his review of his life.

Many people suffered in the Bible, but Job is different. The extraordinary thing about his suffering is not necessarily the extent of it, his innocence or the final end of his travail, but what he *said* while he suffered. Let me explain.

I believe G. Campbell Morgan has it right: There are no answers in the book of Job. The real message is in the *questions* Job asked. Job would be painfully brought to a point in his life where he would ask the most important and pertinent questions in all of the Old Testament - all of them answered in a man he would never meet...Jesus Christ.

In his frustration toward God, Job is pushed to the point where he cries out and asks/makes seven basic questions/statements:

1) 9:2-3 – Can a man be righteous before God?
2) 9:32 – God is not a man as I am...that we should go to court together. Nor is there any mediator between us, who may lay his hand on us both.
3) 10:4-7 – Can You see and understand my plight as a man? Is there anyone who can sympathize with man and deliver him from Your Hand?
4) 14:7-14 – If a man dies, will he live again?
5) 16:18-21 – Is there anyone who can plead for me before God, as a man pleads for his neighbor?
6) 23:3 – Where would I find God to plead my case?
7) 23:5 – How can I know what answer God had sent me?

In his frustration Job finally calls out for God to indict him (Job 31:35-37).

While Job will ask other questions in this book, these seven statements seem to make up the core theme of his desire for God's response. What we discover in these questions and statements is that they are all answered in the person of Jesus Christ. Job didn't know there would *be* a Jesus, but in his despair, he recognized the *need* for one like Jesus.[1]

The story of Job begins to make much more sense to us when we realize how unlikely it is that Job would ask these questions if he had never suffered or felt the extraordinary isolation when everything and everyone had been taken from him.

Job has suffered for all mankind in a unique way. Job was brought down to a few "moments of clarity" that has forever defined the specific needs man has without God. Though Job had faith in God to be righteous, he couldn't see any justice from heaven. Job desperately needed a mediator, a counselor, an arbitrator, and a sympathetic friend who could approach God and plead his case.

I doubt that any of us will ever suffer to the extent Job suffered, but what we all have in common with him is the acute need for a way to make contact with God. We need someone who can both reach down to earth from heaven, and reach up to heaven from earth.

Who else could this be but Jesus?

In the end Job died without knowing why he suffered so much. He died in faith, trusting God to do the right thing.

Here is where the book of Job has relevance for us today. Whatever our loss or affliction, we may never fully see the reason or cause of why we, or our family were victimized. Some evil has an evident source, while other evils are not readily seen. It may be that we will leave this world never knowing why we, or a loved one was afflicted or lost.

But in time, we will discover a small blessing if we can develop the faith and patience as Job.

My brethren, take the prophets, who spoke in the name of the Lord, as an example of suffering and patience. Indeed we count them blessed who endure. You have heard of the perseverance of Job and seen the end intended by the Lord- that the Lord is very compassionate and merciful.

James 5:10-11

Footnotes

1. Scholars believe Job likely lived before Abraham. Job would not then have known about any promise from God for a messiah or savior to bless mankind in delivering men from their sins. Jesus would be *nothing* like the earthly king the people in the first century wanted...but He would be *everything* that Job had asked for.

The rose is sweetest washed with morning dew, and love is loveliest when embalmed in tears.

Sir Walter Scott

Chapter 19

The Paradox of Blessings

Oh my son Absalom - my son, my son
Absalom – if only I had died in your place.
2 Samuel 18:33

At the beginning of Job's trials, he is scolded by his wife and told to curse God and die. His response was: "You speak as one of the foolish women speaks. Shall we indeed accept good from God, and shall we not accept adversity?"[1]

Previously upon receiving the news that all of his children had been killed, Job fell to the ground in worship and said:

Naked I came from my mothers womb, and naked shall I return there. The Lord gave and the Lord has taken away; blessed be the name of the Lord.[2]

Now what on earth does this mean? Am I supposed to just blithely accept the fact that I can't hold on to anything in this life? I need more explanation than this.

Alright, lets try this: think of your life before you met your spouse, before you had children. What was your life like? Wherever you were and whatever you were doing, it was without the knowledge of future blessings. At that time, life seemed full and meaningful …and it was. Yet, as time continued, it became fuller and even more meaningful with marriage and children. You wouldn't want to go back to your former life now; it seems empty in comparison. The paradox here is that the greater the joy - the greater the grief when that object of joy is taken from you. Blessings can hurt.

Now stay with me on this for a moment. It has been said that one of the greatest blessings we have in this life is the ignorance of tomorrow. If we knew the exact day and time we would die, we would in essence be living under a death sentence; mindful of the exact moment of our execution.

Once we had enjoyed the fullness of this life's blessings, if we knew when and how we might lose them, how could we be happy? Further, to know when and how we would lose our spouse or child, would paralyze us with a consuming grief and rob us of every happy moment. We might very well become as Job who cursed the day he was born. Any joy would be fleeting, and life itself would become burdensome and ultimately a cruel exercise in futility.

Here is where Job demonstrates an extraordinary attitude. His recognition of the source of his blessings will not allow him to curse that source, and extinguish any hope.

The joy of material gain is short-lived, but the joy of family will linger through memory. This is a unique blessing that only God could give us through our family. No one can take away that precious moment when your baby looked into your eyes and began to coo; or when your spouse held your hand close to them and declared their love for you; or when your child crawled up into your lap and said, "I love you mommy." These are moments of the purest joy that will live on for decades in our minds.

The extraordinary thing about a life given to us is that nothing else in this whole world can compare to the joy it brings; likewise, nothing else compares to the utter void that comes to us when we lose it. Here is where we may fool stripped of any happiness - yet the Lord has not left us empty. Knowing the Lord will care for our child because our child is *His* child, can give our hearts peace.

What's more, new lives will come to our family. God does not stop creating. If we will accept it, this too is a gift from God. This is the circle of life. There's more to come. We need to wait on God.

Granted, it is painful, but consider: A heart never wounded, is a heart that never really loved.

Footnotes
> 1. Job 2:10.

> 2. Job 1:21.

*The God who put us in our house of flesh,
is waiting to take us outside.*

Chapter 20

Is There Hope in Our Future?

*For I consider the sufferings of this present
time are not worthy to be compared with the
glory which shall be revealed.*
                              Romans 8:18

Hope? Hope for what? To recover my loss? We
can't get it back. We can replace material assets, but
a life that is lost is *gone*; what could we possibly hope
for? Yesterday is over and all of the tragedies that
were a part of it are gone and cannot be recovered.
We could hope for an assurance that this will never
happen again, but that doesn't help us right now.
Besides, we know that all of life is at jeopardy and
the future will likely hold more of the same.

So then why even hope? What's the point?

People use the word *hope* today to mean
everything from a pipedream to a done deal. "Hope"
is all over the map.

The Bible, however, uses hope in a different
way. Biblical hope has no doubt of the final
objective; it will happen, we just haven't *seen* it yet.[1]

Hopeless in Rome?

Most people have heard of Nero, the Roman emperor who reportedly burned down Rome. While Nero was ruling, the Bible warned Christians of the coming persecution that Nero would exact upon Christians. They were warned not to be surprised, nor should they lose heart, but rather rejoice in the trials to come.[2] In a unique way, those trials would help join them to the sufferings of Christ.

I can't imagine the horror these people and their families went through in the first century, but how does their story help me now - in the twenty first century? Yes, I've been impressed with the stories of their courage and faith, but that doesn't mean a lot to me right now as I grieve my loss.

I don't need history, I need a tomorrow.

There Has to Be More

Here is where we hit a wall - a big wall. We've exhausted all the possibilities here and intuitively we know that somehow an answer is on the other side, but we just can't see over it. There *has* to be more than just what we have in this life. Random grief and catastrophic loss cannot be the end of the matter. There has to be some kind of final resolution of all things. You know, like they have at the end of a murder mystery story. Somebody gathers all the principals and explains exactly how and why the crime happened. This is what we want: a revelation, an explanation - a sort of cosmic closure.

I wish I had the answers to these questions. I wish I could go over this wall and look and see the truth to all of our suffering and loss, but I can't. However someone *has* seen over this wall, a man who suffered terrible loss and lived under constant threat of his life. No I'm not talking about Jesus, but another man, a man who was given the opportunity to look over this wall and see the truth of tomorrow. The apostle Paul was likely the man who was mentioned in the Bible as the one "caught up to the third heaven" to hear "inexpressible words."[3]

Your guess is as good as mine as to what Paul saw and heard, but there is no mistake that from that point on in Paul's life, personal afflictions took a back seat to any concerns he may have had for this life. Paul returned with a renewed resolve and wrote:

> Though our outer nature is wasting away, our inner nature is being renewed day by day. For this slight momentary affliction is preparing us for an eternal weight in glory beyond all comparison, as we look not to the things that are seen but to the things that are unseen. For the things that are seen are transient, but the things that are unseen are eternal.

> 2 Corinthians 4:16-18

Hope from an Empty Tomb

Though we don't have full disclosure about what lies beyond the grave, we do have a promise, in writing, from our Creator that assures us He has not forgotten us. And He has proven that promise by raising His Son from the grave. I tell you quite frankly that the empty tomb is the deciding factor for me.

No credible critic denies that Jesus of Nazareth lived, worked, taught and was crucified in Jerusalem. These are indisputable historic facts with corroborating testimonies. The issue for the world has always been the empty tomb.

The Apostle Paul argued that if Christ were not raised - then there is no resurrection; we would have no hope and believers should be pitied by men.[4] The gospel will stand or fall upon this fact.

This is the core truth of man's hope: Christ walked out of His own tomb. Forty days later in a crowd of witnesses, He ascended into heaven. He is now at the right hand of the Father where He rules heaven and earth until death is finally vanquished.[5] This is not my guess, this is my faith…because this is what the Bible says.

The grave is not the end. The chapter in God's book entitled "Earth" will one day be finished. Time will end. Evil will be destroyed. The next chapter in God's book will be written as this new world of permanent, eternal peace will come to all of God's family in heaven. The Prince of Peace will have conquered every enemy. Our Lord will have gathered all of the saints – no one is left behind. The Kingdom of God will be complete. The spirits of just men will eternally co-exist in the very presence of the Almighty Creator and God.

We will see sights and colors we never could have imagined. We will hear a chorus of voices that will astound and thrill us continually. We will now understand the full plan of God. And through it all, we will forever witness the majesty and essence of the King of all Kings...because we will all be there at His feet.

This is the reason I see a future that includes my loved ones. *This* is the reason for my hope...and it can be the reason for your hope too.

Footnotes
1. Romans 8:24,25.

2. 1 Peter 1:6,7; 4:12,13.

3. 2 Corinthians 12:2-4.

4. 1 Corinthians 15:12-19.

5. 1 Corinthians 15:24-26.

A Personal Thought...

When we witness such emotionally charged and life-changing tragedies that come to men, we want to fully understand every nuance of every reason for this horrible event. Even after considering all the dynamics of good and evil, sin and its consequence upon all men and creation, we often still want something more than a cause and effect answer.

We may not doubt the reality of a doomed world, but when we find within this world a small oasis of goodness and innocence, we want to know: Why can't this be left alone? Why can't God shield this goodness from the evil in the world?

<u>Now here is where I offer an opinion</u>:

It may be, in part, that the Lord allows such horrible and evil things to happen as a reminder that this is not what He had planned for us. His perfect world for His children is somewhere else.

We are too much in love with this life. We understandably and naturally surround ourselves with the good things of this life; but it may be that we *need* to occasionally see the raw side of this world as it really is - with all of its brutal violence, all of its destructive deceit, and all of its festering ugliness... *lest we grow too fond of it.*

Epilogue

The objective of this book has been to calm and nurture your troubled spirit, and to present a scriptural perspective of God's relationship with evil in both heaven and earth.

I do not for a moment presume to have satisfied all of your expectations, much less spoken for God. No man has the right or the capacity to do so.

I had a dear friend (now deceased) who was put into the unimaginably dark place of having to conduct the funeral of his firstborn grandson; who grew up in a lawless, drug-addicted world where he eventually took his own life. I asked my friend how he could possibly gather the emotional strength and composure to do what he did? What on earth could you say at a scene like this?

He told me that he cried a lot, he prayed a lot, and then went and faced the audience of family and friends saying: "I don't know what our Lord will do. I do not have the wisdom to know what He *should* do. But this one thing I do know: the God who made heaven and earth won't make a mistake. Whatever our Lord decides concerning my grandson...I know He will do the right thing."

To people of faith, this is where we ultimately leave such matters - in the hands of our Lord, believing that He will do the right thing. Anything else would fall short of any peace we could hope to find in this decaying world.

I pray the things I have written will leave you with a measure of peace and a dawn of hope. May God help us all, and may our Lord bless you and keep you.

"Shall not the judge of all the earth do right?"
- Abraham (Genesis 18:25)

Made in the USA
Charleston, SC
13 January 2017